Political Activism in the Linguistic Landscape

Full details of all our publications can be found on
http://www.multilingual-matters.com
or by writing to Multilingual Matters, St Nicholas House,
31–34 High Street, Bristol, BS1 2AW, UK.

Political activism in
the linguistic landscape

*Or, how to use public space
as a medium for protest*

Along with a *table alphabetical* of
TERMS & CONCEPTUALISATIONS
for the illumination of various pertinent matters

Writ by *Ph. Seargeant*
With *Ko. Giaxoglou* and *Fr. Monaghan*

Sold at the sign of the *Barking Dog*,
St Paul's Churchyard, *L O N D O N*

Political Activism in the Linguistic Landscape

Or, How to Use Public Space as a Medium for Protest

Philip Seargeant

With Korina Giaxoglou and Frank Monaghan

MULTILINGUAL MATTERS

Bristol • Jackson

DOI https://doi.org/10.21832/SEARGE6826

Library of Congress Cataloging in Publication Data

Names: Seargeant, Philip, author.

Title: Political Activism in the Linguistic Landscape: Or, How to Use Public Space as a Medium for Protest/Philip Seargeant with Korina Giaxoglou and Frank Monahan.

Other titles: Political Activism in the Linguistic Landscape

Description: Bristol, UK; Jackson, TN: Multilingual Matters, 2023. | Includes bibliographical references and index. | Summary: "This graphic novel looks at political activism in the public landscape with a particular focus on the UK activist group Led by Donkeys. The book is both an innovative approach to the presentation of academic research, and an exploration of how political activism can use the linguistic landscape as a resource for communicating its message"-- Provided by publisher. Identifiers: LCCN 2023005538 (print) | LCCN 2023005539 (ebook) | ISBN 9781800416826 (hardback) | ISBN 9781800416819 (paperback) | ISBN 9781800416840 (epub) | ISBN 9781800416833 (pdf)

Subjects: LCSH: Communication in politics--Great Britain. | Rhetoric--Political aspects--Great Britain. | Public spaces--Political aspects--Great Britain. | Led By Donkeys (Campaign group)

Classification: LCC JA85.2.G7 S33 2023 (print) | LCC JA85.2.G7 (ebook) | DDC 320.94101/4--dc23/eng/20230302

LC record available at https://lccn.loc.gov/2023005538

LC ebook record available at https://lccn.loc.gov/2023005539

British Library Cataloguing in Publication Data

A catalogue entry for this book is available from the British Library.

ISBN-13: 978-1-80041-682-6 (hbk)
ISBN-13: 978-1-80041-681-9 (pbk)

Multilingual Matters
UK: St Nicholas House, 31–34 High Street, Bristol BS1 2AW, UK.
USA: Ingram, Jackson, TN, USA.

Website: www.multilingual-matters.com
Twitter: Multi_Ling_Mat
Facebook: https://www.facebook.com/multilingualmatters
Blog: www.channelviewpublications.wordpress.com

The policy of Multilingual Matters/Channel View Publications is to use papers that are natural, renewable and recyclable products, made from wood grown in sustainable forests. In the manufacturing process of our books, and to further support our policy, preference is given to printers that have FSC and PEFC Chain of Custody certification. The FSC and/or PEFC logos will appear on those books where full certification has been granted to the printer concerned.

Typeset by R. J. Footring Ltd, Derby, UK
Printed and bound in the UK by the CPI Books Group Ltd

Contents

Setting the Scene   1

A Accountability   8

B Brexit   12

C Covid   16

D Democracy   18

E Emplacement   21

F Freedom of Expression   25

G Grassroots Campaign   28

H Hypocrisy   31

I Intertextuality   34

J Just Joking   37

L Law   40

M Metalinguistic Landscape   44

N Narrative   46

O Online–Offline Nexus   50

P Place (and Space)   53

Q Quotation   57

R Rule of Law   60

S Social Media   64

T Twitter   67

Contents

U   Urban Environments   71

V   Victory?   74

Z   Zed   78

Afterword   81

A Second, More Word-Based Afterword   83

Appendix   86

A Model of Context for Grassroots Political Protest   88

Bibliography   92

Cast and Crew   94

In memory of Jan Blommaert

The linguistic landscape

The ways in which written language
and other semiotic resources are used
in public spaces; and the complex of
social, cultural and symbolic meanings
they communicate.

Setting the Scene

There's an old joke from Czechoslovakia in the 1970s when the country was under Soviet occupation. A protester is standing on the street, holding a blank piece of paper. A Russian official walks up. He stops in front of the man and stares at the piece of paper. 'But where are the letters?' To which the man replies, 'There's no need for letters. Everything is clear'.

This is a short book about language and politics. About the use of language for persuasive purposes in politics – and the relationship between what's said and what's done. There are two planes upon which this use of persuasive language takes place. There are the politicians making pledges, commitments and pronouncements in order to influence the electorate in the hopes of gaining support for their proposed policies. And there are the activists, protesters and media commenting on this use of language, and using their own rhetorical strategies to draw attention to the gaps between the speech and the actions of politicians (or occasionally, in the case of ideologically sympathetic journalists and commentators, to paint over those gaps). This book looks at the latter of these two planes – at the way protesters and activists use language and other semiotic means in an attempt to raise awareness of social injustices, and to hold the politicians who are responsible for these injustices to account.

We can build the scenario that produces these types of protests from the following elements. Politics is about persuasion as much as it is about policy. This is particularly the case in liberal democratic systems, where consent to enact policy derives ultimately from the voters. The ways in which that consent is solicited are, of course, extremely complicated. But insofar as liberal democracies are founded more on open debate than on physical coercion, persuasion is a key factor.

Persuasion can take many forms, and there tends to be a set of beliefs and guidelines within a culture about what constitutes acceptable persuasion and what tips over into manipulation, deceit or other forms of unsanctioned coercion. These guidelines are often partially formalised in regulations covering everything from politicians' behaviour to the conduct of the news media. But regulations are often imperfect for the job they're meant to do, and they can also always be circumvented or ignored. Thus, other forms of critique develop in an attempt to police the line between legitimate and illegitimate persuasion. This takes the form of institutions such as the press, and practices such as activism. Allowance for this sort of criticism is a foundational idea in the liberal model and is often codified in constitutions or bills of rights (the US First Amendment being a paradigm example).

What you end up with are two opposing views attempting to persuade not simply that their own approach or ideology is superior for various reasons – it's more effective, of greater moral weight, and so forth – but also that the way in which the opposing party is communicating their message is illegitimate – that it's deceitful, if not in conflict with the very principles which underpin the democratic system. This type of protest is thus distinctly metalinguistic. Its focus is on how the opposing party is using language and other semiotic means to manipulate public opinion, often through the use of lies or misrepresentation. The fact that the opposition is deceitful in the approach it takes to communication is, so the argument then goes, symptomatic of its members' untrustworthy characters as political actors more generally. So both parties are trying to impose their own narrative onto events, and one way of pursuing this is by criticising both the how and the what of the other party's communication strategy, and by attempting to use politicians' own words and actions against them. The aim is to expose a hypocrisy in these words and actions, which is then presented as emblematic of those politicians' ethical failings, their impaired competence for the job, and their disregard for the principles underpinning the liberal democratic system.

This isn't by any means the only approach to communicating messages of dissent. But it can be a particularly powerful one, and is the focus for the examination of political activism in this book.

***

The other important component for the approach to political activism in the book is the linguistic landscape and approaches to communication in public space. Linguistic landscape research predominantly looks at language in public space: at words, texts and the meanings they generate. But it looks very particularly at the use of this language in its context – as part of the 'landscape' – and at how this context, how place and space, influence the meanings and interpretation of this language use.

(As a side note it's probably worth observing that, as with any discipline, there are debates around how the boundaries of the area of study should be defined, with some people advocating the inclusion of interior spaces or online spaces rather than wholly 'public' spaces, but I will stick here with the more traditional understanding.)

Part of this context – part of the relationship to place and space – is the materiality of the texts: what the signs look like, how they're inscribed in the landscape, their size, shape and all the other aspects of their physical nature. It's perhaps not surprising that linguistic landscape research as a field of study has developed in much the same timeframe as the emergence of smartphone technology has made digital photography such a commonplace part of the fabric of everyday life. Linguistic landscape research is, at its core, a distinctly visual branch of sociolinguistics. It's about the display of language – and particularly written language – in the public sphere. About what this can tell us about the organisation of society. We can add to this the fact that although the term 'linguistic landscape' has become the conventional label for the field of study as a whole, the discipline doesn't constrain itself to language alone. All forms of semiosis are included, from monuments, statues and road signs to the aural and even the olfactory. The linguistic landscape is, by definition, supremely multimodal.

All of which is to say that any discussion of the linguistic landscape needs to embrace this non-verbal nature of the data. And ideally, not simply to discuss it, but also to show it. What follows in this book is an attempt to do just that. It's an examination of one particular way in which the linguistic landscape is used – as a resource for political activism – which aims to tell the story of the research through illustration and visual narrative. Rather than simply including a few photographs as illustrative examples of what's being analysed, the aim is to use pictorial representation as a tool in this analysis: as a way of mapping out the relationship between sign, context and audience which produces meaning. It's not, as most sociolinguistics books are, a verbal treatment of verbal communication, but a multimodal treatment of a multimodal phenomenon.

The research presented in this book was carried out by myself and two colleagues, Korina Giaxoglou and Frank Monaghan, over a couple of years either side of 2020, and sits alongside a long-running interest we have in the expressly political dimensions of the linguistic landscape. The focus, specifically, is on the UK activist group Led by Donkeys, which has, since late 2018, been running a campaign to expose hypocrisy in the political classes. As will be illustrated later, Led by Donkeys started out as four friends who wanted to communicate their frustration over the state of current British politics and thus decided to experiment with putting up satirical billboards among the advertising hoardings in the public arena. As a form of grassroots politics, this activism is responding to a specific political era and operating in a specific political culture. That era is the UK in the second half of the 2010s and beyond. The culture is liberal democracy – that's to say, a democratic system centred around the protection of individual rights and freedoms – as it exists, evolves and is debated in the UK in an increasingly globalised world.

British politics during this time was dominated by four particularly consequential issues: Brexit, Donald Trump, Covid and the Russian invasion of Ukraine. The first of these was a homegrown issue, and the last two global issues which had local political ramifications in countries around the world. The second issue – Trump – wasn't, strictly speaking, a direct concern for British politics at all, other than in the international relations issues it provoked. But such is the cultural influence of US politics on the global imagination, and so stark an example was Trump of the rise of national populist movements and the threat they potentially pose to the tenets of liberal democracy, that it had a significant shaping influence on the cultural landscape in the UK, as it did in many other countries. All four of these became the focus for various demonstrations and political activism in the UK (and, with the exception of Brexit, in many other parts of the world as well), bringing people out onto the streets to protest and to attempt to shift the attitudes and actions of the government. And all four feature in the activism examined in this book. While the central focus is on the exploits of Led by Donkeys, the book also incorporates discussion of examples of similar activism, and the ways in which the linguistic landscape and the use of public space as a semiotic resource plays an important role in this.

The book is structured in the following way. The central component is the visual narrative, which introduces the focus, aims and approach to the research, and discusses the examples, centred around the case study of Led by Donkeys, and the theoretical issues these entail. This takes the form of something approaching a cross between a graphic novel and an infographic, with the visual aspect not only illustrating but also assisting with the presentation of the analysis of the phenomenon under discussion. At times, however, there's a need for a more discursive examination of some of these issues and concepts. Thus, alongside the visual narrative, there's a run-down of key ideas arranged in alphabetical order – keywords, if you will – which also narrate the story of this form of political protest, and the way that it draws upon the affordances of the public sphere. These are presented in parallel with each other, with the pages alternating back and forth between the two. There isn't a systematic alignment between the two at all times, but hopefully the narrative they both individually develop combines as the book progresses to create a coherent whole.

Given that a traditional approach to referencing doesn't sit easily with the visual narration, a bibliography is included separately at the end. The Appendix then draws together many of the ideas discussed in the book into a schema for analysing protest signs. Taken as a whole, these various sections tell of how the linguistic landscape can be used as a communicative resource for expressing messages of critique and dissent, and the role this plays in liberal democratic politics more generally.

7

Accountability

In the context of politics, 'accountability' refers to ways of ensuring that those governing a country act in the best interests of those they govern. It's premised on the idea that those in power have certain responsibilities about how they use their power, particularly when, as in a democracy, that power is entrusted to them by the community at large. If they abuse that power, or fail to carry through on the pledges they've made, they can be held to account. At least, that's the idea.

Accountability has a close relationship with trust and trustworthiness – a trustworthy person being someone who does what they say they'll do as far as this is possible or practical. Trustworthiness is based on being able to predict future behaviour on the basis of past behaviour, and from this, to be confident that a person's pledges are a reliable indicator of what they intend to do. In representative democracies, trustworthiness is thus a fundamental criterion by which a politician is evaluated.

Underpinning all this is an issue about the nature of language. One of the central concerns in the philosophy of language is how words relate to actions, and how this often precarious relationship creates the social reality in which we live. The basic idea is that language – and speech acts in particular – allow for the creation of the social institutions through which our lives are organised. Decisions are made on the basis of pledges, commitments and declarations. It's a faith in the bond between words and actions which gets things done. But the bond isn't a stable one by any means. Lies, manipulation and deceit are all indicators of the instability in this relationship, and all potentially endanger the idea of harmony in society. The concept of accountability is an attempt to mitigate this. It's an ethical notion, the observance of which is built into management systems of all sorts, including the management of a country.

The concept is particularly relevant for the cases looked at in this book in that politics in the UK since the mid-2010s has been dominated by the implications of the result of the Brexit referendum. Although by its very nature a democratic procedure, this produced a political situation in which the normal processes for accountability became disjointed – the Prime Minister who had called the referendum resigned as soon as the result came in, and many of the advocates of leaving the European Union (EU) did not hold political roles that would have given them responsibility for seeing through their pledges. All of which led to a period of political instability.

Four Elections and a Pandemic

A brief chronicle of political instability in the UK

(2015 to 2020)

7 May - The Conservatives unexpectedly win an outright majority in the general election

23 June - The Leave Vote unexpectedly wins the Brexit referendum

24 June - David Cameron resigns as Prime Minister

13 July - He is succeeded by Theresa May

8 June - She calls a snap general election, which results in the Conservatives losing their majority

24 July - Theresa May resigns as Prime Minister

She is succeeded by Boris Johnson

12 December - The Conservatives win a large outright majority in the general election

31 January (11 pm) - The UK leaves the EU

23 March - First UK Covid lockdown begins

Brexit engendered numerous protests and demonstrations

which drew on a host of creative ways to comment on the situation

One of the most prominent was the use of metaphor

HERE LIES BREXIT 2016 - 2019 DIED of its OWN CONTRADICTIONS

Placard from anti-Brexit demonstration

FREEDOM OF MOVEMENT

Participant in the anti-Brexit demonstration in central London on 23 March 2019

responding to the Home Office's announcement that

Or as the Home Secretary (interior minister) Priti Patel put it

WE'RE ENDING FREE MOVEMENT

So people can come here based on their skills, not where they're from

We're ending free movement to open Britain up to the world

B

Brexit

It would be a pleasant daydream to think that one day, in the not too distant future, British politics won't be dominated by Brexit. The reality, though, is that the impact and ideological consequences of the break with the EU that was voted for in 2016 and became reality in 2020 will shape the agenda in UK politics for years if not decades to come. Brexit itself was as much a struggle over self-identity, perceived values and the culture of politics as it was about concrete economic and policy-based issues. But it also came to be about how politics is conducted in the UK, and the role that propaganda and other forms of covert persuasion should play in this.

The issue for us here isn't about whether the UK leaving the EU was a good idea or not, but rather how the process which led up to the decision was conducted. It's about whether this process involved unacceptable levels of manipulation and deceit (the Cambridge Analytica scandal springs to mind here), and where the line should be drawn for what is and what isn't acceptable when it comes to political persuasion. And it's about how the propaganda war then turned Brexit from an abstract idea around concepts of freedom, sovereignty and control into a tribal populist fight.

So while Brexit might, once upon a time, have meant Brexit (as Theresa May so persistently insisted when she was Prime Minister), it also stands as a case study for issues that are equally relevant to countless other political struggles around the world. Take away the details around trading policies and customs unions (which, for many people in the UK, were something they had neither the time nor inclination to fully engage with anyway), and you're left with a conflict conducted almost entirely via the rhetoric of hyperbole which exposes the workings and weaknesses of the political system by which the UK (and many other liberal democracies) live.

But Led by Donkeys developed a different approach

According to their origin story, the four friends,

James Sadri

Will Rose

Oliver Knowles

Ben Stewart

were talking about the chaos that Brexit had unleashed and looking at this 2015 pre-election tweet from the then Prime Minister, David Cameron

David Cameron
@David_Cameron

Britain faces a simple and inescapable choice - stability and strong Government with me, or chaos with Ed Miliband: facebook.com/DavidCameronOf...

07:26 · 04/05/2015

26.1K Retweets 16.8K Quote Tweets 18K Likes

Ed Miliband, former leader of the Labour Party

I voted for CHAOS with Ed Miliband

They discussed the various things they could do with the tweet to make the statement durable and its creators therefore accountable.

They wanted to ensure that 'future historians will know how arrogant and stupid our leaders were'.

They considered printing out the tweet and exhibiting it in a museum,

but finally hit on the idea of blowing it up to billboard size and putting it up out on the streets where everyone could see it.

And so it came to pass

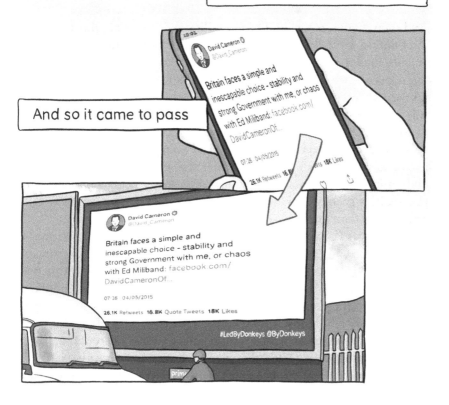

— C —

Covid

And then there was Covid. From a political perspective, this has more in common with Brexit than one might at first assume. The difference is that it was not solely the product of human infighting, but the consequence of a natural disaster, albeit one which a little more far-sighted preparation could have helped contain (and one which was likely linked in some form to long-term human exploitation of the natural environment). Politics entered the equation most explicitly with the response to the pandemic. And even then, the politics of the response was always going to be challenging and involve uncertainty and improvisation. Short of a policy of denial or neglect – of the sort that leaders such as Jair Bolsonaro and Donald Trump flirted with – attempts to contain the disease were often genuine, if flawed.

But it was the way that the Covid response revealed a mixture of incompetence, alleged corruption and discrimination in government circles which stirred up dissent. And the way that, in the UK, this was often startlingly similar to the same issues that Brexit had highlighted about the political system. In the case of Brexit, those who had pushed to leave the EU and those who then used the issue as the basis for their appeal to the electorate held a responsibility to carry through on their promises and assertions. In other words, there was a direct issue of accountability involved – a direct link between what had been promised and what was delivered. In the case of Covid, the accountability was more general and was based on the expectation that elected leaders are working for communal rather than selfish reasons. That the power entrusted in them by the system is not meant to be used for self-gain but for the wellbeing and safeguarding of the electorate.

D

Democracy

All of which brings us to democracy. Or specifically liberal democracy – a political philosophy based around the idea of individual rights, individual liberty, and a government chosen by and accountable to the citizens of the nation.

Democracy, along with concepts such as liberty and equality, are almost taken for granted as the foundation stones upon which political systems in the West are built. There tends to be very little disagreement in mainstream political circles about whether or not democracy is a fundamental good. Disputes about it, at least in mainstream circles, rarely revolve around whether it should be replaced by a different system. Rather, the question is about how best to achieve democratic ideals and address fears of a democratic deficit, how to ensure the checks and balances that support this system are working, and how to worry away at what the concept actually means in practice.

Liberal democracy is traditionally understood to be reliant on two things: the right of people to debate and criticise; and the right to equal and fair participation for all in the system which determines who governs. The former of these has been enshrined in liberal thought since the 18th century. The latter gradually took hold throughout the 20th century. It's the combination of these two which is why propaganda, which can corrupt the fairness of the process of participation, is potentially a problem; and why censorship and restrictions on voicing your opposition, which close down opportunities for debate and criticism, are also problematic. Activism attempts to keep both these as pillars of the social structure, and to ensure that the voice of the governed is not drowned out by the voice of the government.

Emplacement

So we have the system, beliefs about how the system is best monitored and various recent crises which have highlighted the stress points in the working of that system. As noted, communication is fundamental for both the operation and the oversight of this system. And central to all the communication we're looking at in this book is the role played by context.

The reason for this is that, very simply, meaning as it exists in society is always a product of context. That's to say, meaning is something which is interpreted by real people, in actual situations, from acts of communication created by other people, as they interact with the culture and society around them. Language is one of the resources they can use to effect this communication – indeed, it's arguably the primary resource. But the communication becomes meaningful only when it's experienced through the admixture of context.

Which brings us initially to the concept of emplacement. The meaning of a sign is never determined in isolation but is influenced by its location in the physical world. The concept of emplacement is thus concerned with the physical location of a sign and the ways in which that location contributes to the interpretation of the meaning of the sign. Due to a process of socialisation and experience, we tend to have set expectations about the way this relationship between emplacement and sign plays a role in the semiotic process, and these expectations provide a framework in which meaning-making takes place. Working within these expectations contributes to the meaning of a sign in one way, while violating them creates meaning in a different way. A billboard on the side of the road in a capitalist society indexes immediately that its communicative purpose is very likely to be related to trying to sell us something, and we read the content of the billboard accordingly. A billboard which doesn't conform to these expectations about advertising will have been designed to attract initial attention simply by not addressing us as a consumer.

They describe themselves in their book as 'four friends with a ladder' who took on Brexit

But they're four friends with a background in advertising and digital campaigning, and experience of direct political action

And this doubtless influenced the approach they took

Two of them have worked as communication strategists for Greenpeace, for example

The interventions carried out by
Led by Donkeys are linked to various
other types of linguistic landscape activism

from political demos

to graffiti

and subvertising

Freedom of Expression

As we noted when setting the scene, in a democracy, consensus around an issue and the subsequent policy regulating that issue are the product of debate. Ongoing conflict is the natural state for liberal democracy. But that conflict is resolved, periodically and temporarily, through argument and persuasion rather than by overt force and violence. The right to express an opinion, and to attempt to persuade people to accept that opinion, is thus fundamental for liberal democracy, and lies at the heart of the relationship between the government and the governed.

Freedom of expression covers a range of related issues. In the First Amendment to the US constitution, for example, it is aligned with freedom of the press and the 'the right of the people peaceably to assemble, and to petition the Government for a redress of grievances'. The First Amendment thus presents free speech as essential for the viability of liberal democracy because of the safeguards it offers against tyranny from those in power. The right to speak out against the actions of your government is seen as a fundamental part of this type of political system.

The UK has no 'First Amendment' as such, but freedom of assembly is one of the rights provided by the European Convention on Human Rights, to which the UK currently adheres, which asserts that every individual has the right to protest, demonstrate, or march in a public space, regardless of the cause. These rights are not absolute (in the same way that freedom of speech more generally isn't absolute), and can be limited if the authorities deem it is necessary and proportionate to do so. But again, what counts as 'necessary' and 'proportionate' is an issue for debate, and government plans for restrictions on protesting very often become the subject of protests themselves.

These details of and the implications that stem from the legal restrictions placed on the right to protest also form an important part of the context which generates the meaning of any act of demonstration. For instance, an act of protest takes on a different significance if it's likely to lead to the arrest or persecution of the protester. This is perhaps a form of emplacement which considers place at scale. Displaying a protest sign in a public space within a territory which has strict restrictions on freedom of expression creates different expectations for the interpretation of that sign than would the same act of protest in an environment with strong protections of freedom of speech.

But they use a particular cluster of semiotic practices made up of three parts

1. the form of the argument and its political purpose

e.g. Assertions
Exhortations

2. the rhetorical devices

e.g. Wordplay
Slogans

and

3. the sociolinguistic and semiotic means used to communicate this

e.g.
Posters   Placards

Let's look at each in turn and how they apply them

Grassroots Campaign

An important factor in the nature of protest is that there exists a marked discrepancy between the resources available to the government and those available to the governed when it comes to communicating political messages. Those in power have a platform, a prominence and a range of institutional resources at their disposal to facilitate the communication of their message. The public at large have much more limited access to the media of mass communication (even in the age of social media), and thus have to find alternative ways to get their voices heard and their message noticed.

Grassroots protests do, however, have some advantages to compensate for their obvious disadvantages. The advantages relate to the sense of authority they have as authentic expressions of the concerns or will of the people and the moral weight this confers within the context of a democracy. The very fact that a grassroots campaign is *not* perceived as the product of an institution and that it's viewed as a spontaneous reflection of the concerns of real people lends persuasive power to the way it can communicate its message, given the 'for the people, by the people' ideology which permeates popular understandings of liberal democracy.

The value accorded to the idea of grassroots authenticity becomes reflected in both the practicalities and the style of the communication used in demonstrations and campaigns. The Led by Donkeys group, for instance, stresses that its financial support comes entirely from crowdfunding. The money that allows them to stage their interventions is all donated by private individuals and thus they aren't dependent on – nor do they need to be responsive to – institutional backers. Likewise, when it comes to style of communication, grassroots demonstrations tend to predominately feature handmade signs and placards, the material nature of which is in marked contrast to the more polished advertising style of a large organisation. And despite the slickness of the Led by Donkeys' campaigns, they make a great deal in their origin story of the makeshift way in which the whole enterprise began.

Part of all this, of course, is perception and presentation, and there isn't always a clear-cut distinction between institutional and grassroots political communication. Both sides can co-opt the tactics of the other if they think it will be politically expedient to do so. The technique of astroturfing, for instance, whereby organisations pay people to act the part of spontaneous supporters of a cause, is regularly used to simulate grassroots support. Conversely, the interventions carried out by Led by Donkeys often replicate almost precisely the advertising style of the government while at the same time subverting its message. As such, one can see the concept of grassroots interventions as being both a social dynamic involving the political organisation by those without access to established sources of institutional power, and a style or aesthetic which is used to convey authenticity as part of a persuasive repertoire.

Another point worth considering with respect to the way grassroots movements are conceptualised is that, although groups such as Led by Donkeys don't have institutional or establishment backing for their political work, their members nevertheless have a certain status and security within society which provide the foundations from which they can carry out their activism. As has been seen with other activist groups, such as Extinction Rebellion, in recent years, a key resource of protesters in communicating their message is the security they have in terms of cultural and class identity, which means that these actions (such as a willingness to get arrested) don't involve the same level of risk as they might for people struggling with more social precarity.

1. the form of the argument and its political purpose

The idea here is to hold power to account

By looking at the way language is used in the process of governing

Led By Donkeys

IF ONE PERSON BREAKS THE RULES,
WE WILL ALL SUFFER

STAY ALERT 〉 GOVERNMENT HYPOCRISY 〉 COSTS LIVES

Poster in response to the government's handling of the COVID crisis

Mirror
JOHNSON: NO APOLOGY, NO SHAME
Booze, nibbles & party games until early hours
... while the rest of us were cancelling Xmas

The Prime Minister forgetting about the rule against festive gatherings

The Health Secretary forgetting about the 2-metre social distancing rule

The Special Advisor taking his infamous trip to Barnard Castle

IF ONE PEOPLE BREAKS THE RULES

Hypocrisy

What everything we've discussed so far has been leading up to is the issue of hypocrisy in politics. Hypocrisy is very often the result of the way the precarious relationship between words and actions is exploited in political contexts, which can perhaps be most succinctly encapsulated in the mantra 'Do as I say, not as I do'. Norms of acceptable conduct within society are asserted by a politician (either in strict policy terms or as general moral proclamations) and these can then be used to negatively evaluate the conduct of others. These norms tend to be associated with a moral narrative that's firmly embedded within the culture, and gives a sense of authority to the pronouncements. The narrative is then used to suggest that these norms are the natural order of things, on the basis of either tradition or common sense. Yet when, at the same time, those asserting these norms are also themselves violating them, we stumble into the sphere of hypocrisy.

The reason why hypocrisy is the focus of campaigns such as those carried out by Led by Donkeys is that it's emblematic of the violation of the pact between word and action which underwrites the liberal democratic system. Hypocrisy, after all, is to state or pledge one thing and then do something quite different – something which goes against the spirit of the original pledge. In politics it's a close cousin of deceit and manipulation: professing a position in the hopes it will bring political gain while having no intention of adhering to that position when it's no longer expedient to do so. It's a by-product of opportunistic acts of persuasion.

Holding people to account then becomes a process of exposing hypocrisy. Of reminding the public of the past assertions of politicians when these assertions now seem to run counter to present-day realities, and when the politician would otherwise happily deny having made these past assertions.

For those fortunate enough not to have followed some of the more undignified escapades in British politics during this period, a number of government ministers and officials were caught breaking lockdown regulations :

The Prime Minister attended multiple social gatherings when these were banned

The Health Secretary was caught on camera in an extra-marital tangle

The Prime Minister's Special Advisor took an unsanctioned trip up to the north of England when everyone was required to stay at home

Intertextuality

The picture we're building up is one in which hypocrisy, resulting from manipulative uses of rhetoric, is in danger of undermining the ideals of the democratic system, and where activism attempts to push for more accountability in the relationship between the words and actions of those in power. This activism makes use of the linguistic landscape as a semiotic resource, with particular attention to the role played by context in meaning-making.

Which brings us to intertextuality, along with entextualisation and recontextualisation (all the -textualisations, in other words). All three of these are fundamental to discourse creation. To begin with intertexuality, this is a way in which new meaning is assembled from old; in which words and phrases are used for the meaning associated with their previous contexts of use; and in which fragments of discourse circulate within a culture.

In essence, intertextuality references uses of language which originate in, or have become particularly associated with, another text which has accrued a certain cultural relevance. Intertextual uses of language are a form of shorthand, picking up on pre-existing ideas that are salient within the culture. They also operate as a form of community identifier in that their interpretation relies on a particular cultural knowledge. They're often mixed with forms of linguistic or semiotic creativity such as puns, with all this can entail in terms of the attraction of attention. Many of these aspects of the concept can be seen in the design of protest placards, where limited space requires the text to be concise but attention-grabbing.

Intertextuality isn't limited to language alone, however. It can also be used with visual or other forms of communication. The Led by Donkeys' posters which mimic the design of official government posters, for instance, use visually based intertextuality to relate their satirical message directly back to the government's original messages which now form the basis for charges of hypocrisy.

Related to this is entextualisation. When Led by Donkeys take a quote that was spoken or written by a public figure and repost it in the present day on a billboard somewhere, they're drawing on a device that's commonplace in everyday communication. Everyday conversation is made up in part of a patchwork of fragments of discourse which are recycled, recirculated and reframed, as the words and opinions of one person become a ready-made tool to be used (or adapted) by someone else. In basic terms, entextualisation refers to this act of removing a stretch of discourse from its original context so that it can be used for a different purpose in a different context. In other words, the original fragment of discourse is recontextualised, in a new act of meaning-making.

As we can see in the way these related processes are used in the Led by Donkey campaigns, they're ideal devices for highlighting instances of political hypocrisy. The basic technique used by Led by Donkeys is to take a pronouncement made by a politician in the past and expose it to scrutiny in the present: the fragment of discourse is cut from its original context and pasted into a new context; the words remain the same but there's a change in the circumstances which give them meaning.

This change is often the result of the simple passing of time, and the way events that were presaged or promised in the past played out to different effect in the present. By comparing the one with the other – that is, by juxtaposing them – it's possible to highlight the deception, hypocrisy or delusion which led to this discrepancy in meaning. In this respect, juxtaposition is a very simple narrative device that's used to call for more accountability in political discourse.

The juxtaposition takes place either implicitly or explicitly. In some cases, an old statement is re-posed in the present, and the contrast simply comes from the knowledge the audience has of today's political circumstances. No further commentary is necessary. In others, two statements or images are placed side by side, with the first asserting one truth, the second a very different truth.

The underlying belief is that a politician should be consistent in what they say

And a politician who radically changes their views from one moment to the next is, at best, untrustworthy

Just Joking

The 'literary' genre in which interventions such as those made by Led by Donkeys could, very broadly, be placed is satire. The purpose behind the activism is serious, but the approach taken is one of ridicule, of highlighting political cant and disparaging the self-righteousness of people within the political classes. The tone, in other words, tends towards humour, and echoes that conventionally found in public protests, particularly on homemade placards where parody, pastiche and wordplay are used to frame a political message in eye-catching and emotionally appealing ways. This is the use of the joke as a form of defamiliarisation, calling attention to the brazen deceit of political pronouncements through mockery.

The use of public space as a resource for this form of political expression shares this carnivalesque approach, repurposing sites of consumerist communication (e.g. the billboard advert) into ones aimed at critiquing the actions of the establishment.

2. the rhetorical devices

The basic device was very simple

The pledge-as-PR-stunt rarely works out well, as Nick Clegg and Ed Miliband can attest to

But not all pledges are engraved on an 8 foot slab of stone,* so instead, Led by Donkeys decided to memorialize them themselves

FUNDING OUR FUTURE

I pledge...

TO VOTE AGAINST ANY INCREASE IN FEES in the next parliament and to pressure the government to introduce A FAIRER ALTERNATIVE

He voted for an increase in tuition fees in the next parliament

Take a statement a politician had made in the past

and expose it to scrutiny in the present to see how their assertions or promises had stood the test of time

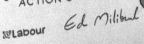

A BETTER PLAN. A BETTER FUTURE.

1 A STRONG ECONOMIC FOUNDATION

2 HIGHER LIVING STANDARDS FOR WORKING FAMILIES

3 AN NHS WITH THE TIME TO CARE

4 CONTROLS ON IMMIGRATION

5 A COUNTRY WHERE THE NEXT GENERATION CAN DO BETTER THAN THE L

6 HOMES TO BUY AND ACTION ON RENTS

Labour   Ed Miliband

* The 'EdStone'

Law

The affordances of the linguistic landscape, when used as a resource for political activism, can be divided into two broad categories. Firstly, there are the purely semiotic resources: the use of billboards, placards, spectacles, projections, graffiti and all the other types of communication which express a message in the public forum. But these alone don't produce the political meaning for the activism – it's rather the way they're displayed within a particular context, and the way this context is drawn on as a communicative resource.

For messages of political dissent – that is, those which criticise the governing authorities – a very important part of this context is the legal restrictions around expressing such messages. As discussed, liberal democracy is, in theory, built on resolving ongoing conflict through discussion, persuasion and periodic consensus. But the parameters for what counts as legitimate persuasion – for how the debate should be conducted – are also a matter for debate. On the one side, this results in arguments about propaganda; on the other, about censorship. In some countries, the parameters in which debate (and thus protests and demonstrations) can be enacted is far more restrictive than in others. In Russia, for example, unauthorised protests were banned in 2014 and violating them can lead to a prison sentence. There are also accounts from Russia of people being arrested for merely tweeting about attendance at protests.

In the UK, the government has recently placed new restrictions on protesting with the Police, Crime, Sentencing and Courts Act 2022. In justifying the need for these restrictions, the government has argued that the 'balance [between freedom of expression and public disruption, as previously legislated] may tip too readily in favour of protesters when – as is often the case – the police do not accurately assess the level of disruption caused, or likely to be caused, by a protest'. In all such contexts, the law, and the way it is used by those in power, is an important contextual factor contributing to the meaning of any act of protest. The law, in other words, regulates not only what can be communicated in the public sphere, but also how it can be communicated. But in creating this type of legislation, it changes the contextual meaning for what is communicated in the public sphere. (See the Appendix for a specific example of this.)

3. the sociolinguistic and semiotic means used to communicate this

And to express this argument they draw on the ways in which the linguistic landscape acts as a form of public communication

The billboard has both practical and symbolic value as a site of activism

John Lennon and Yoko Ono's Times Square Poster

WAR IS OVER!
IF YOU WANT IT
Happy Christmas from John & Yoko

WAR IS OVER!
IF YOU WANT IT

Following the 2017 film 'Three Billboards Outside Ebbing, Missouri'

several activist campaigns used the same format to draw attention to their own issues

17 KILLED IN THEIR CLASSROOMS STILL NO GUN REFORM? HOW COME, PAUL RYAN?

Campaigners calling for stricter gun control following the Parkland School shooting

71 DEAD

AND STILL NO ARRESTS?

HOW COME?

Part of the Justice4Grenfell campaign

M

Metalinguistic Landscape

The metalinguistic landscape is the display, within the public sphere, of language about language. It involves signs which reference other signs, or other public acts of expression. Signs which comment on other instances of public communication, focusing specifically on how these are communicated. In the case of activism and protesting, it usually involves criticising the rhetorical manipulation or misrepresentation that's used by those in power and which, due to the central role that persuasion plays in policy, corrupts the political process.

The metalinguistic landscape can be a linguistic landscape which includes metalinguistic elements or, in some cases, one which reflects upon other linguistic landscapes. Signs which criticise pronouncements that politicians have made in speeches or on Twitter fall within the former category. Signs which criticise the way politicians use the public space as a resource in their own communications fall within the latter.

In both cases, the rhetorical technique used by the protesters is to focus on how politicians are using language in what is, according to the protesters, an illegitimate or deceitful way, as determined by ethical norms within society. So while the metalinguistic function in Roman Jakobson's original conception included acts such as conversational repair and clarification for effective communication ('Sorry, I didn't quite catch your meaning there. Would you mind explaining in more detail?'), here it's primarily to do with the norms or standards of communication expected in political discourse within the context of the local political system.

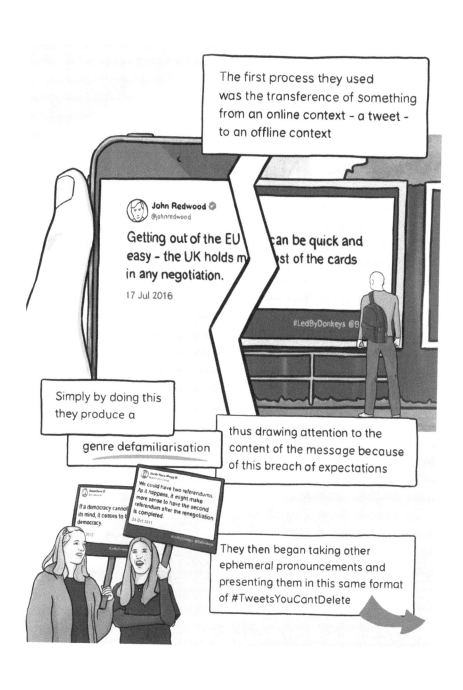

Narrative

When used in politics, the word 'narrative' usually has a double meaning. The first is a variant on its core, conventional meaning: a story which explains how and why events happen in the way that they do. The second is something akin to ideology: the belief systems that shape that explanation. The two are intertwined. A political narrative is ideologically driven – in fact, it's a vehicle for a particular ideology – while at the same time offering an explanation in the form of an overarching story. The desire to have this story adopted as the accepted version of events, or as the common-sense explanation of why things are happening in the way that they are, is what's behind the desire to 'control the narrative'.

The storytelling part of political narratives involves the use of a discursive structure which creates a narrative effect. At the heart of classic conceptions of what constitutes a narrative is the idea of change. Something happens. As the literary theorist Tzvetan Todorov put it, a story moves through three stages: from a sense of equilibrium at the beginning, through a period of disruption, then back again to a renewed sense of equilibrium. This change, in whatever form it takes, has implications for our understanding of the world. It may threaten our wellbeing, make us question our beliefs, or demand some sort of response. Most classic storytelling is based around this formula: a moment of change followed by the struggle to respond to it.

The rhetorical device at the centre of Led by Donkey's actions is based simply and directly on this premise. In other words, their posters are structured as very concise narratives. When they began adding a gloss about the original source of the quotes they were using, they signed off each poster with the rhetorical question 'What changed?' The purpose of the posters themselves was to highlight a perceived change in attitude or behaviour by the politicians responsible for running the country which suggested that the original statement had been disingenuous, deceitful or deluded. The narrative at the heart of each of their posters was based around a contrast in behaviour. A contrast between then and now, between what was said and what was done, between the expectations raised at one point in time, and the reality being experienced at another.

The second definition of narrative in politics is also inherent in the work Led by Donkeys do. They began as an anti-Brexit protest group, and this is the political ideology that shapes their interpretation of events. But the focus of their work has tended to focus on the values that underpin the workings of liberal democracy, and how these can be corrupted by politicians. This could, in theory, be applied to politicians of any political allegiance. During the time that Led by Donkeys has been operational, however, only one party has been in power in the UK and thus the focus has mostly been on it.

In one case, they put up a billboard quoting a speech by the Conservative MP Jacob Rees-Mogg

He was an ardent pro-Leave campaigner, and an implacable opponent of a second referendum

In 2011, however, he had said

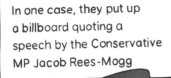

'We could have two referendums. As it happens, it might make more sense to have the second referendum after the renegotiation is completed'

Led by Donkeys duly printed his words in Twitter format on a giant billboard

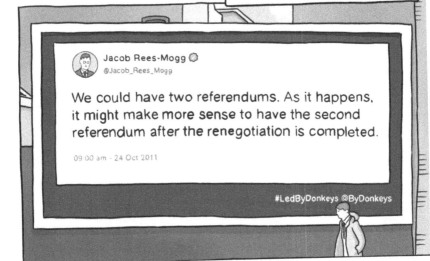

Jacob Rees-Mogg
@Jacob_Rees_Mogg

We could have two referendums. As it happens, it might make more sense to have the second referendum after the renegotiation is completed.

09:00 am - 24 Oct 2011

#LedByDonkeys @ByDonkeys

But Rees-Mogg was able to deny he had ever tweeted these words

which was technically correct

So they added a disclaimer for cases like these

ake more sense to
n after the renegot

24 Oct 2011

He didn't tweet it, he actually **said** it!
In the House of Commons. **What changed**?

#LedE

But the disclaimer also acted to re-emphasise their point

He didn't tweet it, he actually **said** it! *bold*
In the House of Commons. **What changed**?
context → ↖ *question*

The use of **bold text**, the citing of the context, and the question 'what changed?' all draw further attention to the underlying hypocrisy

Online–Offline Nexus

The interplay between the online and the offline worlds is vital for modern political activism. A major way in which this manifests itself is through the options for visibility offered by social media. In today's world, spectacles are often staged in real life in order that they can be filmed or photographed and then broadcast online. As so often with the influence of technology, this practice itself isn't new – but it happens at a pace, frequency and scale that were never possible before.

In the case of political protests, the interplay between the offline and the online magnifies and circulates the message. But the Led by Donkeys posters derive an important part of their meaning and impact from their physical dimensions and location. It's the very fact that they're understood as real posters plastered up on the side of real streets which gives them a status and storyline which wouldn't exist if they were online only.

The majority of the audience for the posters won't witness their concrete physical nature directly, however. The audience who experience them 'in the flesh', as it were, will amount to a few thousand who happen to pass through the location in which they've been posted. It's because they're photographed, uploaded to social media and shared that they're widely seen. Importantly, then, the way in which they're photographed – and specifically the framing of them as part of the wider social streetscape (often with passersby as part of the composition) – is important in conveying this physical reality even as it's via the online space that they make their greatest impact.

The technique is usually just to take the remarks from one context and place them in another

There's no commentary around them

They're simply left to speak for themselves

Boris Johnson ⊘
@BorisJohnson

It's the arrogance. It's the contempt. That's what gets me [about becoming Prime Minister without an election].

21 Jun 2007

He didn't tweet it, he actually wrote it!
In the Telegraph about Gordon Brown becoming PM.

Boris Johnson ⊘
@BorisJohnson

[It's] a transition about as democratically proper as the transition from Claudius to Nero. It is a scandal.

21 Jun 2007

But sometimes they use a juxtaposed entextualisation

These were put up just after Boris Johnson had become prime minister himself without a general election

For example, they take two statements from the same politician

2016

and place them next to each other

Chris Grayling ⊘
@ChrisGraylingMP

There will be a free trade agreement that allows all our business to trade freely to and from continental Europe. It will take a relatively short period of time.

2016

he actually said it!
how on the Andrew Marr Show.

2017

Chris Grayling ⊘
@ChrisGraylingMP

These are going to be lengthy negotiations, they're going to be challenging negotiations. Nobody has ever said the negotiation would be straightforward and simple.

17 Oct 2017

so that the discrepancy between them acts as its own commentary, highlighting the hypocrisy of both statements

The juxtaposition of two images to create a short but striking narrative is something they've continued to experiment with

A nurse in the NHS

Duty

The prime minister and friends at a Christmas party during the Covid lockdown

Duty free

Led By Donkeys

But now, the contrast between the images is accompanied by a one or two-word commentary

which uses parallelism and wordplay to further reinforce the point

A socially-distanced Queen at the funeral of Prince Philip

Selfless

Self-serving

Led By Donkeys

A social gathering of the Prime Minister and his colleagues which took place at much the same time as the funeral

Place (and Space)

Traditionally, definitions of place and space have seen the former as more of a cultural phenomenon, the latter as more of an abstract phenomenon. Space relates to geographical location, whereas place relates to the meanings which that location has for people. It's how people think about a point in space, how they perceive and use it, the role it plays in their community, and the way this complex of meanings shifts and is constantly contested. This results in what Doreen Massey refers to as a 'sense of place' – the various meanings attached to a location by people.

Technology invariably alters the understanding and experience we have of place, particularly in the way that globalisation has brought about forms of time–space compression whereby online spaces are able to collapse the geographical distance between places. One of the implications of this is that it leads to different ways of identifying with place, allowing us to play a part in both the environs in which we're physically located, and distant communities with which we can interact with almost equal ease.

Ideas of both public space and place are important for the linguistic landscape in that meaning is influenced by the simple facts both that the signs are located in public forums and that the particular locales have their own complex of cultural meanings.

An obvious point in this regard is that signs placed in the public sphere are almost invariably addressed to the public – that is, to anyone who happens to encounter them as they move around that space. The signs are indiscriminate as to audience, unless certain provisions are made to exclude some groups – for instance, through choice of language or the inclusion of specific terms of address. And the fact that they anticipate a public audience means they tend to address this audience as a community.

Arguably, anything and everything in the linguistic landscape is political simply by virtue of its public nature. Public space is always regulated in some form or other. Signs are used to denote ownership or oversight of the space, to display the codes and laws which regulate behaviour in that space. They can be used to revolt or protest against these regulations, and to mark the identity of the different people and groups who live in that location. It is natural, then, that public space itself is used as a resource for explicit expression of political opinions, and that the affordances of the linguistic landscape are drawn upon by demonstrators.

The other important role played by place is that it often sets up a dialogue with the intervention. The cultural symbolism for the UK of the Houses of Parliament or Buckingham Palace, for instance, creates a potent counterpoint for a message about political corruption, as all the ideas, values and history associated with the two places becomes part of the context in which the intervention's message is interpreted.

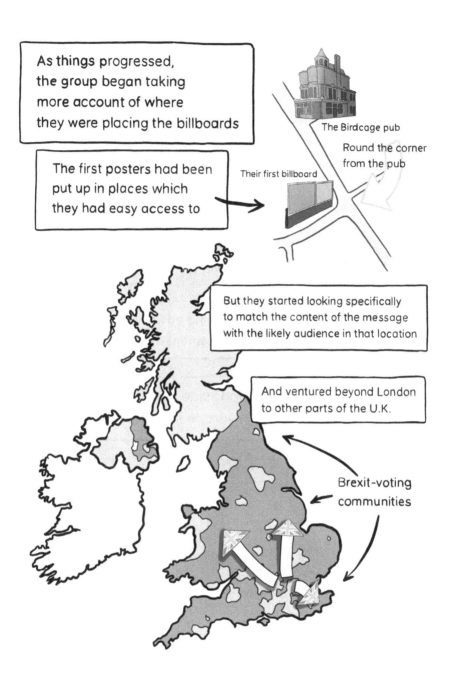

As things progressed, the group began taking more account of where they were placing the billboards

The Birdcage pub

Round the corner from the pub

Their first billboard

The first posters had been put up in places which they had easy access to

But they started looking specifically to match the content of the message with the likely audience in that location

And ventured beyond London to other parts of the U.K.

Brexit-voting communities

The juxtaposition of message and place was further exploited

when they began using advertising vans, which could be repositioned in specific contexts

For example, running alongside Nigel Farage and his 'Brexit Betrayal' march in 2019

Quotation

Quotation is the attribution of an opinion, and the way it's expressed, to a specific person. It's a particular form of entextualisation, whereby the original fragment of discourse is explicitly framed as having been spoken by someone else, and this attribution becomes an important part of the context in which the utterance is interpreted. As we see with the Led by Donkeys posters, it is the direct relationship between person and utterance which acts as the anchor for the meaning that the posters generate.

In many scenarios, the relationship between utterance and person can be used to convey some form of authority – either through the authenticity of the source, or via some form of expertise conveyed by their status. The use of quotations in academic writing, for example, is usually for this purpose. In combative political discourse, on the other hand, the purpose is less to do with authority than with account-ability. A quote whose genuineness and accuracy can be evidenced by published or recorded documentation becomes a hugely useful resource for creating a narrative which illustrates expedient uses of rhetoric for political gain.

They built on this juxtaposition of place and message when they began projecting images and films onto famous landmarks

Buckingham Palace acted as the backdrop for an exposé about Boris Johnson's lies

The White Cliffs of Dover became the background for a film about asylum-seekers

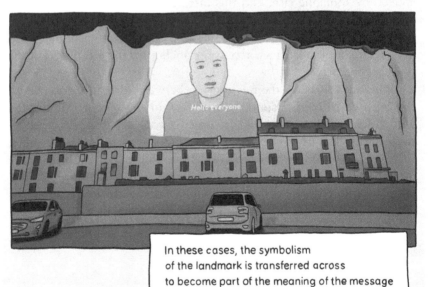

In these cases, the symbolism of the landmark is transferred across to become part of the meaning of the message

Led By Donkeys ✓
@ByDonkeys

Art, activism and accountability 🐴. All our work is funded by the public. Want more? Become a regular supporter or make a one-off donation 💧. DMs open 📩.

📍 United Kingdom 🔗 donate.ledbydonkeys.org 📅 Joined December 2018

Following   Followers

Place is also important when they post photos of the signs to social media

Led By Donkeys ✓ @ByDonkeys
A national embarrassment

(Location: Dagenham)

This shows quite how important the relationship between the online and the offline is for the success of the project

Both the spectacle and meaning come from the physical artefact and its placement in a specific location

But its impact is as much to do with the way it's photographed, circulated on social media,

Totally f⬛king hopeless
11:23am ✓✓

Boris Johnson describing Matt Hancock who he repeatedly refused to sack, even after he broke his own lockdown rules.

Led By Donkeys

and is seen by an audience unconstrained by time and space

R

Rule of Law

In our earlier discussion of the linguistic landscape and the law, we looked at how legal regulations around forms of public expression created different contexts in which the act of protest itself is interpreted. To put it crudely, there is a great deal more at stake for someone involved in a public demonstration where such demonstrations are outlawed and punishable by incarceration or even death than there is for someone living in a society where this is not the case. But issues related to the law can, and are, also used as part of the content of protest messages.

With the onset of the Covid pandemic there was much talk in the media and among political commentators in the UK of the 'rule of law' – the concept that all members of society, whatever their status or identity, are subject to the same laws, and that this too is a fundamental principle of liberal democracy. With incidents such as Dominic Cummings's trip to Durham during lockdown* and the various parties held at 10 Downing Street while social-distancing regulations were still in force across the country, the accusations were that the government was violating the very laws that it had introduced.

The same basic principle concerning speech acts and hypocrisy applies here as it does to other forms of political persuasion, only with more explicit institutional force. Any law is a decree about expectations of behaviour within society, but one which has the institutional backing of the state. The expectations about behaviour are expressed

---

* Dominic Cummings was, until late 2020, chief advisor to Boris Johnson during his time as Prime Minister. In early 2020 he was accused of breaking the government's own lockdown regulations by travelling with his family from London to Durham in the north of England.

verbally (i.e. written into law) but can be enforced by various other means (the threat of incarceration, for example).

Government responses to these specific accusations were that they'd only unwittingly broken the rules (Boris Johnson's defence about the Downing Street parties) or there had been extenuating circumstances (Dominic Cummings's defence about the need for his trip to Durham). The contention from their side was that it was an issue to do with interpretation of the parameters of the law rather than one to do with the more substantive issue of rule of law itself. From the perspective of their critics, these arguments were deficient in two ways. First was the strong suspicion that the arguments were disingenuous – that the politicians in question fully understood the implications of their actions yet went ahead regardless. Second, even if there were some truth in the excuses, ignorance of the law is never usually an acceptable defence for breaking it, and issues of accountability should apply here just as they do in other walks of life.

Another part of the context is
who is responsible for the messages.

Some of the devices used by Led by Donkeys
are increasingly used for political communication
by governments as well as activists

The MI6 building
in London

February 2022

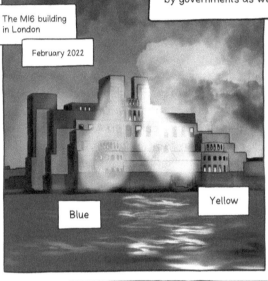

Blue

Yellow

After the invasion of Ukraine in February 2022,
for example, landmarks in cities across the world
were lit up with the colours of the Ukrainian flag
as a symbol of solidarity

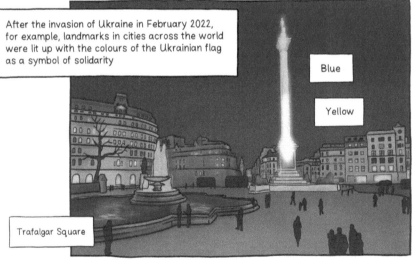

Blue

Yellow

Trafalgar Square

But the meaning is very different
when the author also has
real political power to effect change in the world

There was criticism that in a
situation like the war in Ukraine
symbolism simply wasn't enough

Expressions of moral support were no substitute
for decisive political action of some sort

Social Media

We have noted already that social media can be an important tool for political activists in terms both of the help they can give in organising groups and events, and for the publishing opportunities they offer. The networked nature of social media makes it relatively easy to establish connections with like-minded individuals, to set up and communicate with groups, and to coordinate the actions which constitute the activism. Likewise, the speed and scope of social media's publishing reach allow for the wide circulation of activists' messages.

For the approach taken by Led by Donkeys, however, there's another very important way in which social media have made an impact on public discourse. This concerns the way that digital communications technologies have altered certain elements around the ontology of language use. The introduction of digital communications platforms altered the default for acts of communication from predominantly ephemeral to predominantly permanent. Anything communicated online – especially on social media platforms – has the potential to be stored indefinitely and circulated endlessly. Related to this is the way that online communication can be replicated with great ease, and then passed on or recontextualised. And finally, online texts are searchable, and thus utterances from the past can be easily located and retrieved. For a rhetorical strategy which consists of raising awareness of politicians' past remarks, such as that used by Led by Donkeys, these affordances provide an ideal toolkit.

For their part, Led by Donkeys produced a tour of London

highlighting places in the city that are used for the laundering of oligarch money

The writer Oliver Bullough explaining how the 'London laundromat' works

As well as other forms of semiotic parody

A blue plaque to mark the presence of one of the most high profile oligarchs in London

Brexit may have dominated British politics in the late 2010s But it wasn't the only source of political hypocrisy

A welcome message for Donald Trump on the occasion of his state visit to the UK

And as we've seen, Led by Donkeys have looked to confront other examples of corruption, deceit and bigotry

Their response to attacks on the Royal National Lifeboat Institution for rescuing boats carrying asylum seekers across the Channel

Twitter

We can focus this down even further. Led by Donkeys is a group particularly associated with one specific social media platform. The brand it first cultivated was centred around the tweet. In doing so, it drew on two elements of Twitter. First was the distinctive look of the tweet and its genre as a short, written public statement. Second was the symbolism that has developed around the platform as an emblem of a particular strand of modern public discourse.

The format has various advantages for the aims of the group. It's graphically simple: a short line or two of text, a small avatar of the author along with their name, and the date on which the message was posted. In other words, it has all the key context about who the comment was made by and when, and in addition the brevity of the format fits nicely into the genre of the advertising billboard. It also creates a sense of genre defamiliarisation when what is usually seen on the small screen of a phone gets pasted up on a billboard that is 14 foot by 48 foot.

Then there's Twitter's influence on public discourse. When Elon Musk was first thinking of purchasing the platform in April 2022, he asserted that 'Free speech is the bedrock of a functioning democracy, and Twitter is the digital town square where matters vital to the future of humanity are debated'. Which has an element of truth to it (even if Musk's concept of free speech would come under a great deal of scrutiny in the months that followed his eventual purchase of the platform). Journalists tend to be on Twitter and so the platform plays its role in setting the news agenda. It also provides a slightly grey area between the off-hand comment and the statement of record, and prompts questions of whether there's a difference in status between the two as far as accountability goes.

There's also the issue of what impact Twitter is having on the style of political discourse. Its format not only lends itself to provocative statements, the simplification of issues and abusive rhetoric, but this is arguably a fundamental strategic part of the business model, in that encouraging this type of interaction plays well in the attention economy. This coarsening of debate under the influence of social media, not to mention the whole issue of 'fake news', has been much debated in terms of the state of politics today. All of which provides a contextually resonant framing device for Led by Donkeys' message.

In late 2020, they collaborated with the Covid-19 Bereaved Families For Justice group

to create a memorial for those who'd died during the pandemic

and to call for a public enquiry into the government's mis-management of the health emergency

The result was the

National Covid Memorial Wall

The wall is covered with tens of thousands of hearts

along with messages of remembrance in a host of different languages

Sometimes people embedded material aspects of the wall into the messages

Like this drawing of a heart around a crack in the wall, with the message,

'My heart is broken'

Urban Environments

Linguistic landscape research has traditionally looked mostly at urban environments, given their population density (over 80% of the UK population live in urban areas) and concentration of social institutions. Urban centres also tend to be the sites for political protest, given the symbolic and practical role they play in the running of the country. Occupying space and displaying messages in the heart of the city is likely to attract maximum attention and create maximum interruption. But again, although the physical manifestation of Led by Donkeys' posters is placed in a particular urban setting, the audience for it can be a fully national (or indeed international) one, given the way spectacles of note get picked up by the media, both traditional and new.

The symbolism of place is also crucial for the Covid wall

It runs along the front of St Thomas's Hospital

where Boris Johnson was treated when he had Covid

THE NATIONAL COVID MEMORIAL WALL

It stretches from Westminster Bridge to Lambeth Bridge

And looks out across the Thames to the Houses of Parliament

Palace of Westminster

Thames

Covid Memorial Wall

The Covid Wall may look like a change in tactics

But it shares many of the same features that are found in all their protests

- There's the sense of spectacle
- The symbolism of location
- The interplay of online and offline
- The targeting of political hypocrisy and ineptitude

And the use of the public space to do all this

Parliament Square

David Davis
@DavidDavisMP

If a democracy cannot change its mind, it ceases to be a democracy.

9 Nov 2012

#LedByDonkeys @ByDonkeys

We didn't tweet it, he actually said it!
In a speech 'Europe: it's time to decide'. What changed?

V

Victory?

So what effect does all this have on the political direction of the country? Attempting to gauge the actual impact that activism has is always difficult. If the initial intention of the interventions by Led by Donkeys was to stop Brexit being passed into law, then it clearly failed. Occasionally, protests which have a very specific sets of aims can succeed in getting a decision reversed or halting an initiative. But more often than not, the intention of the activism is less about direct concrete consequences and more to do with raising awareness of an issue, pushing it on to or maintaining its presence in the public agenda, so that it becomes part of the context when other parts of the political system are deciding on the direction of policy.

In the case of the broader aims of the Led by Donkeys group, these are firmly rooted in the need for accountability in the political community, and its campaigns work as a check against abuse of power. In the end, Boris Johnson resigned as Prime Minister after mass resignations from his cabinet and public expressions of criticism from his parliamentary colleagues. The reasons they gave for the loss of confidence in his leadership were concerns over the lack of integrity in the decision-making, which had led to the scandals over his and others' behaviour during the pandemic. These were precisely the issues that Led by Donkeys had been highlighting in its interventions. It's not possible to measure precisely the influence that the group had in shaping the climate which ultimately led to Johnson's resignation. But we can say that its activism was a highly visible element of the public critiques that aimed to hold Johnson accountable for the behaviours which did, ultimately, presage his downfall. And in this respect, perhaps the best way to gauge the success of activism of this sort is to consider what the political environment would be like without these sorts of projects.

In other words...

Z

Zed

As we reach the end of the alphabetical run-down of key terms, it's worth perhaps reflecting once again on the way that meaning is manufactured by context, and the role played by public place and locale in this. And looking in particular at the way that this applies to political symbols, and their use as part of the wider repertoire of semiotic resources that get mobilised for political communication.

Political symbols can be created from just about anything. Back in 2013, a penguin briefly became the symbol of anti-government protesters in Istanbul. When violent clashes between the police and protesters initially broke out, the national TV channels all chose *not* to cover them. The programmers on one of these channels, CNN Turk, chose instead to run with a wildlife show about penguins – which were then adopted by protesters as an emblem of their struggle.

It's the context in which symbols are used, then, and the interpretation they prompt in their audience, which gives them their depth of meaning. The linguistic landscape, at its most basic level, comprises a context in which the rules and norms which impose some form of order on society are communicated to the public. We can read the concerns of a culture from the linguistic landscape, track the history and identity of the local community, the prevailing belief systems and their stress points from it. And very often, the best picture of society comes from the interplay between 'official' and grassroots interventions in the linguistic landscape.

The use of symbols, whatever their provenance, is a fundamental part of any political conflict. It's part of the propaganda strategy that tries to shape the public narrative. If we take, for example, Russia's invasion of Ukraine in February 2022, the war for public opinion that ran alongside the actual war gave rise to a host of symbols representing support for one side or the other. Twitter and Facebook were full of people who'd added the Ukrainian flag emoji to their name. The defiant words of the Ukrainian defenders of Snake Island – 'Russian warship, go fuck yourself!' – became a powerful underdog slogan, appearing on placards at demonstrations, and even became the basis for an official Ukrainian postal stamp.

On the other side, the most notable symbol was a simple Z. This came to represent support for Russia's invasion of Ukraine. It was painted on the side of tanks; emblazoned on the shirts of Russian gymnasts; and incorporated into the spelling of place names such as КуZбасс in south central Russia. In some countries, the Czech Republic for instance, there were discussions about whether displaying the symbol should be a criminal offence in the way that other forms of support for the Russian invasion were.

There was a great deal of discussion in the media at the time about *why* this had become a pro-war symbol, and what its origins might be. Was it because it represented the Russian word for 'west' (*zapad*), the direction in which Putin's tanks were rolling? Or was it shorthand for *za pobedu* – 'for victory'? Then there's the oddity that the Cyrillic alphabet doesn't have a sign resembling Z. The *zed* sound is written з.

The use of letters of the alphabet as political symbols is a little unusual for the simple reason that individual letters aren't meant to have any intrinsic meaning of their own. They're supposed merely to represent sounds, which, when combined, produce words which do have a meaning. When the NATO phonetic alphabet was being developed, for instance, one of the criteria for words used to represent letters was that they should 'be free from any association with objectionable meanings'. In other words, they should be politically and culturally neutral, in the same way that the letters themselves are.

The neutrality of alphabetic letters was also behind the World Health Organization's decision to use Greek letters to designate new variants of Covid. Prior to this, the variants had been named according to their place of origin – but this produced the danger of stigmatising locations or countries by having them forever associated with the virus. Even then, certain letters had to be omitted in case they accidentally led to unwanted associations. The letter *xi*, for example, was skipped as it resembles the surname of the President of China, Xi Jinping. Language is always political at every level.

It's not surprising that the two most recent instances of alphabetic letters as political symbols – Q, for QAnon, being the other one – have adopted the least used of all the letters in the Latin alphabet. Z is both the last letter of the alphabet and has traditionally been seen as superfluous. Q is likewise distinct from many of the more popular letters, while also having associations with words such as 'query' and 'question'. Neither, then, is a complete blank canvas upon which people have imposed a meaning.

But ultimately, it's the way that signs are used that transforms them into symbols. It's a matter of who they're used by, and for what purpose. And once this usage begins to spread through society, being adopted by supporters, highlighted and debated by the media and, in some cases, banned, its meaning quickly gets embedded in the culture, until it becomes part of the vocabulary we use to make sense of the world, and becomes part of the context which identifies partisan viewpoints and contributes to the war of propaganda which lies at the heart of all political activity.

As we've seen with other examples in the book, those same tactics used by grassroots activists can be used by the political establishment, and indeed by authoritarian regimes.

A question that always arises with protests and activism
is what tangible effect they actually have

Despite all the highlighting of hypocrisy
the government still pushed its Brexit bill through
parliament

The government has continued to cling to power (even
if several prime ministers have come and gone)

And at time of writing, the UK has recorded more
deaths from Covid than any other European country

So what, in the long run, have groups
like Led by Donkeys achieved?

Perhaps we can give the last word to Hannah Arendt, who wrote that

'No one has ever doubted that truth and politics are on rather bad terms with each other...

Lies have always been regarded as necessary and justifiable tools not only of the politician's or the demagogue's but also of the statesman's trade'

But just because it's been ever thus, this doesn't mean we shouldn't still be calling out this behaviour whenever we come across it

And exploiting the semiotic possibilities of public space

to spark a public conversation can be a very powerful way to achieve this

LIAR

Led By Donkeys

A Second, More Word-Based Afterword

When working with the publisher on the blurb for this book, they suggested calling it an 'experiment' in alternative ways of presenting research. In one way, this is an accurate enough representation. One of the purposes of the book has been to break from the conventional strictures of academic writing and try out alternative means of approaching the reporting stage of the research procedure. The very concept of academic writing, along with the baroque institutional practices that can be involved in getting that writing into print, have become so entangled in the last few decades in a mix of socially, economically and politically motivated conventions that the basic purpose of creating a readable text which reports upon interesting and noteworthy ideas or findings in an epistemologically sound manner can all too often become obscured. It's a depressing state of affairs to think that modern academia has produced an environment in which scholars feel compelled to spend two or three years of their life producing something which is unlikely, simply because of the set-up of the current system, to find an audience of any great size. It's against this background that the idea of experimenting with alternative ways of presenting research – and particularly ways which try to engage their readership in an innovative manner – seems like something worth attempting.

So how does an approach like the one taken with this book relate to the conventional tenets of research presentation and academic writing? The research for the project focused on a simple question: how can people who are engaged in political activism draw upon the affordances of public space and the linguistic landscape to communicate their message? The research process involved a variety of different sorts of data. Firstly, there was the online archive of the Led by Donkeys interventions, which can be easily accessed from the group's social media accounts. Secondly, there are reports of their actions – the book they wrote, newspaper and television interviews with them – which offer discursive accounts of their activities and professed intentions. Thirdly, there is the political background: the archive that exists of political statements relating to the issues singled out by Led by Donkeys, as well as the media discourse around this. All this data is textual (much of it multimodal), and analysis involves examination of the discourse, drawing particularly on theoretical concepts from linguistic ethnography (e.g. entextualisation, emplacement, etc.) to explore ways that discourse-in-context aims to influence people's perceptions of events. But as has been reiterated throughout the book, the interplay of temporo-spatial context and sign is central to the meaning-making process, and thus the research also involved physical interaction with the geography of the linguistic landscapes discussed in the book, with a view to recording the phenomenological experience produced by the protests. At the very beginning of the visual narrative, we place ourselves, as researchers, in the frame as it were, as a means of investigating and illustrating that very concrete relationship between place, space and meaning that generates the type of communication we're discussing.

So the approach focuses on the value produced at the interface of the linguistic and the landscape, on the way that place provides a ready-made meaningful cultural context upon which the texts themselves can draw to create their own meaning. We do this by identifying techniques used to shape the messages of the texts themselves, looking at how these reference local and global culture, and how the emplacement of the texts exploits environmental meaning. Alongside this we also take a narrative approach to how the techniques were developed over time, how experiments with media (projections, billboard vans, etc.) allowed the group to adapt their core ideas for different environments, and how the brand that they developed facilitated larger and more ambitious projects. All of this seemed to fit well with a format centred around visual storytelling. In using this format, some of the normal paraphernalia of academic writing had to be omitted, and a subsequent challenge would be to consider how the citation-heavy style of the modern monograph might be married with elements of this book's approach. But that's for a future experiment.

Appendix

Analysing protest signs

Two protest 'signs', both from 2019, from the U.K. and Russia

Appendix

One of the main focuses of this book has been on how the linguistic landscape is used as a resource for expressing messages of political protest. There are two main aspects to the linguistic landscape which are fundamental to its use for this purpose: the fact that it's public; and the contextual meanings that signs derive from this publicness.

Over the next few pages I sketch out a model to help with the analysis of the way meaning is derived from the contextual factors which have a bearing on signs in the public sphere. Signs derive their meaning from the manner of their expression, their situatedness, and the cultural background against which they're presented. These three categories can then be broken down into more specific factors. Manner of expression involves genre, register and materiality; situatedness involves place space and audience; cultural background involves politics, culture and law. Each of the categories which comprise the model can play a part in influencing how the meaning of the sign is interpreted, and each can thus be turned into a question which can then be used in the analysis of the way protest signs work.

In the diagram on the following page, the questions are grouped together under nine headings in the inner circle. The question we can ask with respect to materiality, for instance, is what is the physical appearance of the sign, as this then has a bearing on how we interpret its message. In the two examples on the following pages, answers to these questions for the two protest signs are ranged around the outside of the circle.

The examples are both from 2019. The first (the man carrying a sign saying 'Our crowd is bigger than yours') is from a demonstration that occurred when Donald Trump arrived for a state visit to London, on the invitation of the then Prime Minister, Theresa May. The second (a mock grave for Vladimir Putin) is from a wave of protests in Russia following the introduction of restrictive new laws about regulation of the internet and a clamping down on forms of dissent.

Most of the categories of context listed in this model for interpretation are dynamic. They're liable to change, as other cultural and historical currents change. But it's through marshalling the meanings offered by this dynamic context that protest can engage with issues of immediate consequence in society as and when they rear up from the politics of everyday existence.

A model of context for grassroots political protest

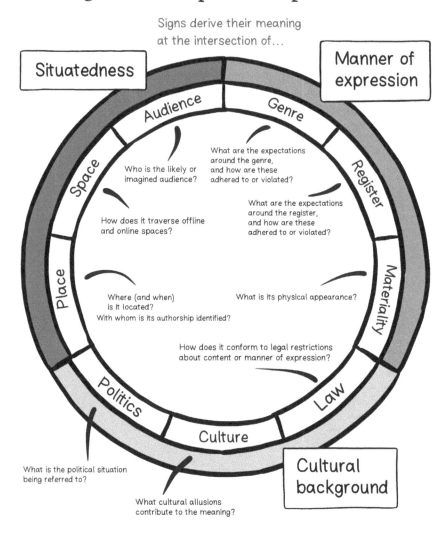

Signs derive their meaning at the intersection of...

Situatedness

Manner of expression

Cultural background

Audience — Who is the likely or imagined audience?

Genre — What are the expectations around the genre, and how are these adhered to or violated?

Space — How does it traverse offline and online spaces?

Register — What are the expectations around the register, and how are these adhered to or violated?

Place — Where (and when) is it located? With whom is its authorship identified?

Materiality — What is its physical appearance?

Law — How does it conform to legal restrictions about content or manner of expression?

Politics — What is the political situation being referred to?

Culture — What cultural allusions contribute to the meaning?

The protest was covered by the news media, as well as images from it being widely shared on social media. So although its symbolic location was the centre of political power in the UK, it also spread across a national and international space

There is nothing particularly notable about the register in this case; instead it relies on other factors to attract attention and generate meaning

The phrasing of the sign addresses Trump directly, and the organisation of the march was meant to coincide with his visit to Downing Street, so that he could, plausibly, witness it directly. But the audience is also the UK political classes, plus the population more generally

The genre is a standard demo placard, complete with slogan and image

The genre is a standard demo placard, complete with slogan and image

Situatedness

Manner of expression

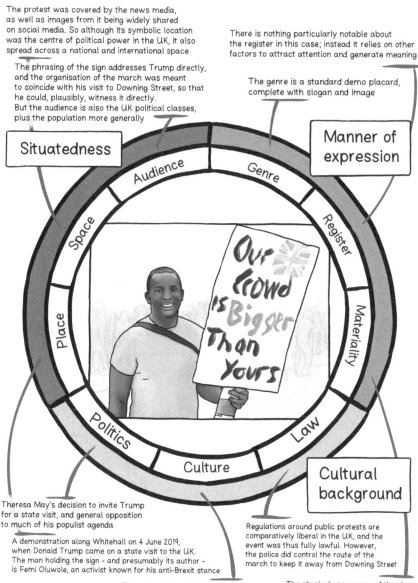

The protest placard reads: "Our crowd is Bigger Than Yours"

Cultural background

Theresa May's decision to invite Trump for a state visit, and general opposition to much of his populist agenda

A demonstration along Whitehall on 4 June 2019, when Donald Trump came on a state visit to the UK. The man holding the sign – and presumably its author – is Femi Oluwole, an activist known for his anti-Brexit stance

Regulations around public protests are comparatively liberal in the UK, and the event was thus fully lawful. However, the police did control the route of the march to keep it away from Downing Street

The cultural allusion here is to Trump's insecurity about the smaller size of the crowd at his inauguration compared to that for Barack Obama

The physical appearance of the sign is very much handmade, in keeping with the idea of grassroots protest

A protest group named Bessrochka then posted about the grave, along with their condemnation of the new laws, on social media. It was picked up by the international press, thus moving from a very localised space to a global one

The register is appropriate for the genre, with only Putin's name, his dates (the second one imaginary), and portrait included

The audience is likely both the authorities, and others concerned about the new legislation

The genre is a mock gravestone, with only the content - Putin's name and photo - indicating that it's not genuine

Situatedness

Manner of expression

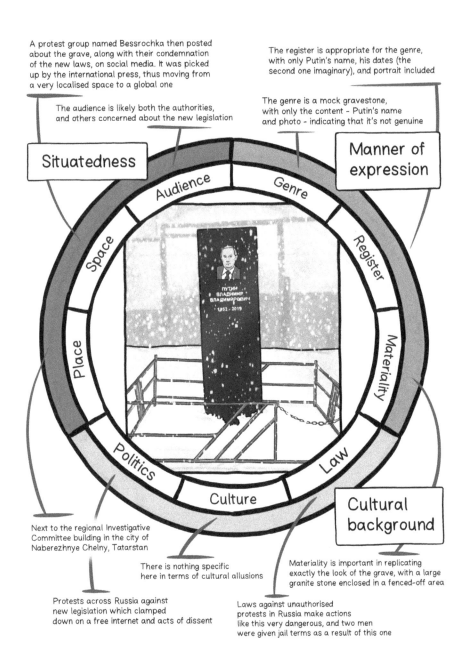

Audience

Genre

Space

Register

Place

Materiality

Politics

Law

Culture

Cultural background

Next to the regional Investigative Committee building in the city of Naberezhnye Chelny, Tatarstan

There is nothing specific here in terms of cultural allusions

Materiality is important in replicating exactly the look of the grave, with a large granite stone enclosed in a fenced-off area

Protests across Russia against new legislation which clamped down on a free internet and acts of dissent

Laws against unauthorised protests in Russia make actions like this very dangerous, and two men were given jail terms as a result of this one

One final word on context...

... on the 'linguistic' landscape ...

... and on signs

The common sense assumption is that signs use language, or maybe visual symbols, to say something

And that context then contributes to how people interpret these words or images

But sometimes the complete absence of words can also be a powerful sign in its own right

A woman is arrested for protesting with a blank sheet of paper under Russia's strict anti-demo laws, Nizhny Novgorod, March 2022

Bibliography

Arendt, H. (1967) Truth and politics. *New Yorker*, 25 February, http://www.newyorker.com/magazine/1967/02/25/truth-and-politics (accessed 12 March 2022).

BBC News (2022) Elon Musk warned he must protect Twitter users, 26 April, https://www.bbc.co.uk/news/business-61225355 (accessed 12 March 2022).

Beeman, R. (2010) *The Penguin Guide to the United States Constitution*. Harmondsworth: Penguin.

Blommaert, J. (2013) *Ethnography, Superdiversity and Linguistic Landscapes: Chronicles of Complexity*. Bristol: Multilingual Matters.

boyd, d. (2014) *It's Complicated: The Social Lives of Networked Teens*. New Haven, CT: Yale University Press.

Briggs, C.L. and Bauman, R. (1992) Genre, intertextuality, and social power. *Journal of Linguistic Anthropology* 2 (2), 131–172.

Jakobson, R. (1960) Linguistics and poetics. In T. Sebeok (ed.) *Style in Language* (pp. 350–377). Cambridge, MA: MIT Press.

Jaworski, A. and Thurlow, C. (eds) (2010) *Semiotic Landscapes*. London: Continuum.

Kramsch, C. (2021) *Language as Symbolic Power*. Cambridge: Cambridge University Press.

Led by Donkeys (2019) *Led by Donkeys: How Four Friends with a Ladder Took on Brexit*. London: Atlantic Books.

Lou, J.J. (2016) *The Linguistic Landscape of Chinatown: A Sociolinguistic Ethnography*. Bristol: Multilingual Matters.

Massey, D.B. (2005) *On Space*. New York: Sage.

Pennycook, A. and Otsuji, E. (2015) Making scents of the landscape. *Linguistic Landscape* 1 (3), 191–212.

Phillips, W. and Milner, R.M. (2020) *You Are Here: A Field Guide for Navigating Polarized Speech, Conspiracy Theories, and Our Polluted Media Landscape*. Cambridge, MA: MIT Press.

Przeworski, A., Stokes, S.C. and Manin, B. (eds) (1999) *Democracy, Accountability, and Representation*. Cambridge: Cambridge University Press.

Pütz, M. and Mundt, N. (eds) (2019) *Expanding the Linguistic Landscape: Multilingualism, Language Policy and the Use of Space as a Semiotic Resource*. Bristol: Multilingual Matters.

Radio Free Europe (2019) Mock Putin gravestone lands two Russian activists in jail, 12 March, https://www.rferl.org/a/russian-jailed-over-mock-gravestone-reading-putin-1952-2019-/29817033.html (accessed 13 March 2022).

Scarvaglieri, C., Redder, A., Pappenhagen, R. and Brehmer, B. (2013) Capturing diversity: Linguistic land- and soundscaping. In J. Duarte and I. Gogolin (eds) *Linguistic Superdiversity in Urban Areas: Research Approaches* (pp. 45–74). Amsterdam: John Benjamins.

Scollon, R. and Scollon, S.B.K. (2003) *Discourses in Place: Language in the Material World*. London: Routledge.

Searle, J. (2011) *Making the Social World: The Structure of Human Civilization*. Oxford: Oxford University Press.

Shohamy, E. and Gorter, D. (eds) (2009) *Linguistic Landscape: Expanding the Scenery*. London: Routledge.

Todorov, T. (1969) Structural analysis of narrative. *NOVEL: A Forum on Fiction* 3 (1), 70–76.

Tufi, S. (2013) Shared places, unshared identities: Vernacular discourses and spatialised constructions of identity in the llinguistic landscape of Trieste. *Modern Italy* 18 (4), 391–408.

UK Government (2022) Police, Crime, Sentencing and Courts Bill 2021: protest powers factsheet, https://www.gov.uk/government/publications/police-crime-sentencing-and-courts-bill-2021-factsheets/police-crime-sentencing-and-courts-bill-2021-protest-powers-factsheet (accessed 12 March 2022).

Vaidhyanathan, S. (2018) *Antisocial Media: How Facebook Disconnects Us and Undermines Democracy*. Oxford: Oxford University Press.

Winberg, O. (2017) Insult politics: Donald Trump, right-wing populism, and incendiary language. *European Journal of American Studies* 12 (2), 1–16.

Zimdars, M. and McLeod, K. (2020) *Fake News: Understanding Media and Misinformation in the Digital Age*. Cambridge, MA: MIT Press.

Cast & Crew

Written and illustrated by
Philip Seargeant

Based on research conducted with,
and additional material written by

Korina Giaxoglou

and

Frank Monaghan

CPSIA information can be obtained
at www.ICGtesting.com
Printed in the USA
JSHW061137050723
44237JS00002B/117